Trying to Catch a Flame in this Windstorm at the End of the World

Poems

Steve Henn

ARROYO SECO PRESS

Logo by Morgan G Robles

Arroyo Seco Press

www.arroyosecopress.org

Cover art: Luke Henn

ISBN: 979-8-9918724-3-0

Poems

What if I tell you, you are not different
it's the family albums that lie
—will any of this comfort you
and how, how should this comfort you?

—Adrienne Rich

Do yourself a favor
Become your own savior

—Daniel Johnston

I. Security Blankets

On a Day I'm Wondering *What*
the Hell is the Point Anyway?

My mom's been paying a lady
to help with laundry and dishes and cleaning
the bathroom ever since I got
divorced, even after my ex-wife died.

I might as well make all the confessions.

I pick at my fingernails incessantly,
rarely use a trimmer. I drink sometimes
76 ounces of Coke in one day.
It's probably too easy to teach adequately;

I'd rather not make the effort
to be all-world about it. Thirteen years
left, coasting toward retirement like
a twelve-year-old on a longboard.

Some of these days, the whole day is
bitter. God knows how debilitating
morale will be by then.

I hear the young teacher across the hall,
my former student, newly married,
turning cynical. He sounds like me.

Please God, don't let him ever
get divorced. Bless him, grant him
the Grace of satisfaction in his work.

Just a few years ago he sat in the front
row, would call out "Hey Henn,"
and ask what I thought about anything.

Please Lord, give him and his wife,
who teaches in the EL Department,
beautiful, beautiful, beautiful babies,

give them astonishingly beautiful children,
to whom no harm will ever come.

Hail Mary
after Frank Ohara

for Anne Henn

Mothers of America!*
Take your boys to the library!

Introduce them to the pleasures of reading
so they don't mature into 40-year-old
overgrown adolescents
who still play "smear the queer" and give each other
purple nurples!

Show them adventure and excitement that can all
be experienced safely, between the ears!

It's true we need adults
who can fix stuff
and beefy security guards

for "an evening with" concerts featuring
some washed up popstar or group
from an ancient decade,

but it would also be nice, 30 or 40 years from now,
if our President had literacy skills!

They'll stop bouncing basketballs incessantly
against the kitchen wall
and scampering up the stairs
like they live in a zoo

for they'll be too busy
using context clues to decipher what "ameliorate" means

or writing poems for their 2nd grade crushes
with the empathy and self-awareness of people who've
experienced
the minds of others

rather than vandalizing on Halloween
                    or sneaking vapes
                              or snorting pixie stix for practice!

If they like reading, you'll have paid it forward into the fund
          whose dividends are your-boy-is-becoming-a-better-person

                    and if they don't like reading
                         they'll get really into sports
                              or crushing things
                    or become officers in their local INCEL chapter!

*so don't blame me if you don't take this advice***

                    and more wars are started, more women are abused
                              and they all learn to drop bombs with
drones

into enemy wedding parties from a remote locale using a joystick
                              that functions like a video game
controller

                    and feel guilty when they're old for all their toxic mistakes
                              or even worse: not.

* a line from Ohara's "Ave Maria"
** also a line from Ohara's "Ave Maria"

a Small Reckoning *or* Bob-O-Matic

When I was in middle school
there was a janitor named Bob
who everybody called Bob the janitor
who would pick up change
off the floor when he spied any
lying about in the cafeteria
or in the corners of the carpeted hallways

and so what happened was, boys —
this type of thing was always done
by boys — began sticking fishing line
with rubber cement or a piece of chewing gum
to a quarter or sometimes a whole dollar bill
and leaving it three or four human measures
away on the floor next to their table
in the cafeteria or in the hallway, a few strides
from where they stood, a group of tweener boys
plotting hilarity, keeping an eye out
for a victim, or for The Victim, the one

they hoped for — other kids noticed of course
and would ask what they called this advanced
pranking technology and they'd say it's called
a Bob-O-Matic, it was the easiest thing
to understand, everybody understood the gag
of ridiculing the old, hapless, underpaid janitor,
too poor to retire, too spry for death, who
wiped their unnecessary ketchup spills
off their lunch tables and who picked up
their intentionally discarded used Kleenex's
from the hallway floors

Everyone roundly agreed that Bob-O-Matics
were hilarious, especially the boys, all of us
boys, all of us pissants laughing and high fiving
over the imagined insult that Bob the janitor
never fell for, though many of the boys said they
got him, many of the boys had their moment
of cruel glory in an imagination that would grow
into adulthood, in an imagination that was just
beginning to get warm.

The Dumbest Boy in Class

Mr. Torrence loved me
for answering every History question
and I have to admit I was eager
to answer every History question
never thinking once about why
these other kids weren't even
bothering to read the textbook

and because I craved his approval
desperately I devised a system
for cheating with my best friend-
bully-frenemy whereby I would hold
a # of fingers on the back of my head
each collection of digits corresponding
to A, B, C, or D and we did
amazingly well on those multiple
choice History tests, Mr. Torrence
even pointed the two of us out
with compliments and thanking us
for studying so hard

                      but I was a chump,
not a class hero, taken advantage of
by an opportunistic pal who always
seemed to manipulate things
to his own advantage such as when
we both traded baseball cards of
our own, bartering together with his
quasi-stepdad for a truly rare
truly valuable 1950s Satchel
Paige card which somehow worked
out to be his alone when we grew
older, or the time a year after
high school, I drove home
from upstate New York, gave him
$500 to buy a bulk amount
of that typical barely adequate
Mexican weed to sell and he

probably saved my ass by taking my money
but when he told me he was held
up at gunpoint by gangsters he
laughed long loud and bursting
as if he couldn't even bullshit
with a straight face I had no spine,
I just took it, I fucking played along,
like he'd actually lost the money,
fuck 19-year-old me, and so

in fifth or sixth grade too namby-
pamby to stand up for myself
we did the digital hand code
a second time except he'd told
everyone how it was and
Mr. Torrence was so pleased
and really taken aback that
our whole class had pretty
much aced that collection
of facts about how the Pilgrims
and Indians got along so well

and so in that way once again
I proved myself the dullest
tool in that proverbial box
which was a classroom
full of nascent sociopaths
where I was only just beginning
to make a fool of myself
with my dunce cap
and my through-the-roof
IOWA standardized test scores
and my desperation
to be loved unconditionally
by other 11-year-old kids

My Debut

I performed in drag once.
I was the Church Lady
for our K-6 Catholic school
talent show. Doing my best
Dana Carvey doing prudish
judgmentalism to the goofiest
degree, and I admit

when I pulled up the purple
skirt over the opaque hose
and slipped the purple jacket
over a white blouse, donned
a pair of genderless black shoes,
then the wig newly sprayed
silver, lifted off a styrofoam
bust onto my head, affixed
with pins by my mother

it was thrilling, putting on
such a get up to do comedy
that made the first and second
graders roar in fun, or incred-
ulity, I admit it was a great thrill
to perform anything, *although*
dressed as a woman or
because dressed as a woman —
who knows? I was twelve

and it felt wide, not deep
like getting the popsong goose
bumps on my arms and thighs
in the back of my frenemy-
bully's mother's minivan
tuned in to top 40 U93, and it
only occurs to me now (over
half a life later) that bully-
bestie-frenemy started
calling me "Stephanie"
somewhere around then

to emasculate me and it worked,
I hated it and after all I was
kind of a pansy — all nearly-six-
foot of me, so I didn't fight back,

when he pinned me on the playground
and shoved his crotch in my face
I lay limp, waiting for him
to grow bored, and when he
twisted our legs into a scissor-
hold I didn't resist much
when he'd torque and flip
me on my back mimicking
what was called "pro
wrestling" on TV, I thought

it was all pretty stupid,
I just wanted to be the
cool kid's best friend,

and I remember now "Stephanie"
began when I ridiculed him
for reading Nancy Drew books
and he came back at me
that biographies of Abraham
Lincoln were stupid and
then the unwanted, overt
feminization, so
one morning I stayed home
from school begging vague
illness and I even made myself
feel real vertigo when I sat up
needing to be sick so badly
terrified of my life
and for two straight weeks I hunkered
by a glass of 7 UP continuously
refreshed by my mother beside
the plate of saltines I precariously
survived on, begging
whenever I was reduced to
begging not to be sent
back to that hornets' nest

I had convinced myself
all the boys I thought
were my friends hated me
and was I even wrong
about that?

Fort Wayne Sport Club Travel Soccer, a tournament in Ohio, Summer 1993

I wish I could remember it
frame by frame. Center-left,
nearer to the center field circle
than the half moon atop the 18.
I'm not exaggerating. Let me
have this. I think I was dribbling
to the left. Head down. Did I
glance at the goal, so far off,
at their enormous keeper,
several inches past 6 foot?
I did. Absolutely launched
The ball with my left foot —
my stronger leg — just lifted
through it with an extravagant
follow-through, hit the pitch
on my backside wildly, head
up, watching. Listen. This is
no fish-that-got-away. All of this
was once possible, once happened.

From the ground, head up,
watching the ball beeline,
then knuckle. He didn't expect
it to carry so far — a step too close
to his right hand post, he dove
a fraction late to his left, and —
I swear to God this is true — as
his right hand reached the ball knuckled
over it, then ducked into the upper corner,
side netting, opposite where I lay splayed.

My teammates crowding, all of us
jumping, a pack of ecstatic 17-
year-old boys, and Pat was screaming
What?! What?! and laughing
And Jesse was shouting *I can't
believe it! I can't believe it!*
That was it. That was the moment
I'd give away whole pieces of myself
to play again. Once upon a time,
I had a body that could do this.

Latte Interlude

it is raining and 50 degrees
    in June so cold but I am not depressed
in the coffeehouse reading again

          I don't know what else
  to do with my life

          Dave G shows up
a person infiltrating this poem

"What's good" he doesn't say
        in so many words I tell him I am trying

to make books happen in unlikely places
               wishing for a local friend

        who writes — of course this summer is full
of notebooks —

      God Bless this merry coffee house tho
          it gives me somewhere to go

      God Bless Tim who owns and runs it
God Bless Indiana ambivalent tho I am about her

      Land of my Birth, may Grace
          somehow change you

Poem for Austin, the Boy Who Threatened to Kill my Son on Social Media

Luke played two parts in the school play,
a comedy about Greek mythology. Achilles,
the nearly indestructible warrior, and Man,
as in kind. If you could've seen how authentically
he accepted the manhood granted by Prometheus,
how knowingly he popped the footrest on the
dadchair stage right, cheekily commanding
Pandora to "make me dinner, woman!"
If you could've seen how happily
he flitted Trojan to Trojan,
touching each with a plastic sword
so they'd swoon and fall and die like straight men
playing dead as only brothers would,

perhaps you would've clapped,
or laughed, or as you sat there
scowling while a boy you insist
cannot be a boy carried himself
proudly across the stage in lights,
perhaps you would've understood
how unnecessary it is to threaten
another child on Instagram, how you
never actually had to message him
to insist he could never be
the one thing he's always —
in his heart's core, in his heart
of hearts — known himself to be.

Raised on Grease and Child Abuse
after Aimee Nezhukamatathil

for June session summer school kids 2017

They'd point at my penny loafers and
my black Tiger Basketball sweater and call me
Poindexter. This went on for a while. I didn't
respond to their threats. The big kid
terrified me — giant white trash boy,
greasy hair, his father beat him,
he survived on McDonalds cheeseburgers and crystal
Pepsi, I don't know, whatever. I didn't feel
for him, he terrified me. The runt
with the orange hair I ignored. But after they
talked and talked about beating me up
one of these days off the bus (me: mute,
terrified, telling no one, hoping
it just wouldn't happen), the little ginger
with the rat tail stalked me past the bus stop,
a series of jabs to my midsection
which didn't hurt me or bowl me over.
I just stood there. Let him hit me. If I had it
to do all over again, I'd elbow smash his face.
Then the big boy pushes the orange boy
out of the way, says *no, this is how you do it*
and wallops his fist into my eye. That's it.
That's the fight. I bent over crying
and a friend from the neighborhood walked me
home, saying, *you're going to have a shiner!*
Later, my dad told me, *sometimes
you've just got to hit back.*
But I've never hit back. Not once
in my 46 years have I ever hit back.

heads of state

I wish we had a special name
for our governor instead of governor.
Something like "czar" but not that
crazy. If we put it to a vote
the winning title would probably be
"Coach." We've got statues
of John Wooden and statues of Lou
Holtz. *Oh boy, Beav,*
do we ever love our kindly
authoritarians! I'll say!
Before you start canonizing
our heads-of-little-s-state
remember that Mitch Daniels
once flashed his "President of Purdue"
credentials to get out of a traffic
stop. Now imagine what laws
he ignored as governor.
I'm sure even Birch Bayh
might've had some weird sex thing
buried deep — he didn't even act
on it, but it was in his head
and here in Hoosierland we judge you
even for that. "Administrator"
wouldn't do it. Neither "Teacher"
or "the Reverend," thank the Lurd,
as my 2nd-least-favorite priest, from Mishawaka,
used to call Him. We should probably just call
him — the governor has never not been
a "him" here — *the Grand Poohbah.*
That's who my dad took me and my younger
brother hunting for on car adventures, in, oh,
1982, or -3. An honest guy, a regular guy,
someone you might chat with over a beer
if you happened to catch him at the
JustLikeUs Bar, hanging out with a throng
of Everymen. May the Lurd bless him
and keep him, the Poohbah was reliable.
We always found him at the Dairy Queen.

Any American High School

When the first period bell rings
one of the assistant principals
chimes in on the P.A.
with the obligatory moment
of silence followed by the
Pledge of Allegiance.
Everyone stands.

From that point on, rest
assured, we take great care
to indoctrinate no one. We do require
they stay at one desk for
the duration; raise hand
to speak; follow instructions;
use the e-hall restroom pass app
when they muster up the courage
to ask permission for their
bodily functions. Thank goodness

we don't spend that time
indoctrinating. The Army recruiter
sets up tables at lunch.
A local pastor is welcomed in
to counsel a child he's cleared
to talk to. Every afternoon there's
fitness training for the JROTC.
No indoctrination here, thank
the lucky Lord. Once, a man
came to be celebrated for his
participation in the Iraq War.

He said the enemy over there
isn't too bright. He said
it'd take 3 or 4 of them to add up
to the brains of one U.S. Armed
Forces man. A child asked a question
from the audience and he said
"I'm not a politician."

Thank goodness no one at that speech
nor anytime after was subjected
to indoctrination. Some mornings
the Fellowship of Christian Athletes
"gather round the pole" at 7:20,
just in time to show everybody
driving their kids or riding in buses
that they're darn good nationalists
conflating their country with
religion. They're doing
the right thing. Doing things
the way they're supposed
to be done. Don't let anyone
ever tell you the Good Lord
doesn't bless this nation.

High School English Teacher

Some days you feel like a pointless taskmaster
haranguing a gang of disaffected devotees,
late bell to late bell. Some days you wonder
if anything coming out your own mouth
makes sense. Some days you don't want
to be here at all. You're eyeing the clock
as the minutes float by, the students schlump
out of the room. Tic . . . tic . . . you wander
too easily off topic, too uninspired with yourself
to maintain merely a bad mood, not nearly
a healthy negativity. Some days you ask
should I be doing something else?

Other days you slog through hours of two-paragraph
responses hoping for a spark in the thinking
to fire you up, to stoke a response. It doesn't
always happen often but it happens not never
too. One day you get an email from a former
student praising you, the best teacher
he ever had, including college too. You're happy that
he thinks the challenge your course presented
sent him crawling up a hill of language
to another level of skill. There's nothing much
to say back about this. Thank him,

What else can you do? When you drank
a lot you might've seen a former student
at the bar who insisted on buying you a beer,
you might've listened to the boozy truth
of how they honest-to-god loved you.
Your dream is to be flown across the country,
around the world even, to read your poems
to honestly interested crowds of eager
listeners, but this is what you got instead:
about 25 faces per class period, hopeful,
or bored, or angry, or sad, somewhere else
in their heads or right here, right now,
turning the light of their young and, yes,
you know it to be true, their hopeful,
their eager faces toward you.

While Birds Sing

Sometimes I look up
across the backyards, past trees,
between neighbors' houses,
and there seems a shimmer to everything,
less like a halo than like a computer
screen, as if it's all matrix,
programming plugged into us
like so much magic, like a life
more movie than life, but so long
between moments of plot complication.

The blur is softer in the early
evening, it may be
the dust of the Sahara they say
was and is and can be blown
across the ocean to reach us
here in our version of the Center
of the Universe. Maybe what's

real isn't optical — perhaps
there's a reality beyond which
we can see and hear and feel,
something beneath the pixels,
something behind the puzzle
pieces, something constant,
and comforting, and wholly
believable, like the magic

of photosynthesis, like
the only mentor I've ever
really trusted will be waiting
to greet me, like he'll be there
inside the light of the final-
Final when I finally make it across. . .

Awareness Level: Eleven

There's a tunnel at
the end of hope. All
my chances at love
slurp down
that way in fits
and starts like
the dregs of a blended
mocha. I'm starting
to go off on dudes
but mostly on my
self. Dear God,
Dear Jesus, Whoever,
I'm starting to wonder
If I can take 20, 30 more
years of this. Lord, don't
give me what I want.
Just yesterday I dreamt
I really met a woman
of intrigue so now
I'd like her to materialize.
Beam er down, Scotty.
Make her lonely and
a writer, like me.
Make her someone
I can swap poems with,
writing all night
together. "Try this…"
she'll say, reading my
poem, and I'll read hers
and say "This is great!"
and I'll really mean it.

II. Snoopin'

Adult Basic Education

My Dad would listen to classical music in the car,
From some radio station at the bottom end of the frequencies.
He called the pop radio I knew so well, and loved so well,
Sometimes imagining my love for it to be a secret,
"I love you so much I got the dry heaves." It was
One of his running jokes. My Dad had a lot of jokes.
His favorite two things to say were "they can't all
Be winners" when we didn't laugh and "I got
A million of em!" when we did. Dear God, do I wish
He would've stayed. For several rides in the Buick
Century he bought foolishly in bipolar mania at
Sticker price from the fucking Petro Brothers
Car dealership, he prodded me to volunteer
To teach adults to read in a local program known as
Adult Basic Education. He must have meant it to be
For my benefit. He must have hoped for a mentor for me
Who might understand me better than he did.
I was selfish as any 12-year-old, not gifted
With an inordinate compassion, and declined.
"Inordinate" is a word my dad would use
As was his favorite, "asinine." He only called
Other adults he imagined foolhardy or unintelligent
Or self-interested "asinine." Each time he asked
If I would grant my time to someone who needed help
And each time I said 'no' or 'no, thanks' or 'not really
My thing' until he quit asking. What would've happened
If I'd've said yes? Would he have stayed? Would he have been
Entirely too proud of me to vanish as he did?

Jack's Gettin Up There

I told Jack I don't know
if I'll make it to 70 and
he laughed and then he didn't.
Jack's gotta be 80. Once
in class some kid asked him
what Vietnam was like
and he said "a real picnic."
He's got a crusty exterior
but a heart bigger'n' a wooly
mammoth's. I fear the day
he dies. I fear it like
I fear the death of my own
mother. It would be
wonderful to let go
of the fear. It would be
so beautiful, not to be afraid.

a Funeral

There was a lotta Jesus stuff at the funeral
that's what they do at Methodist funerals
lots of Jesus stuff 'free' Methodist why free?
Are there Methodists in chains?
Are there Methodist supremacists?
There's a young black man here
and a black older woman and a dark Asian
Indian woman bobbing like buoys
In this lily-white sea of grief
my best friend would say "It's a funeral don't
make it about race" as if I'm Arlo Guthrie
cracking jokes about father-rapers at a women's shelter
in some places punchlines don't fly, they sink
dark bowling balls in unsilly unsalty seas
this preacher doesn't know the woman he is eulogizing
well and that makes the day harder for my friend, her daughter
is anything in this brief vale not ridiculous?
When somebody dies can we maybe
put someone up to speak about her who
knows the names of her children?

The Poor Kid

We were going to have a rumble
during recess, the idea of fighting
made me nervous, at the moment
it went down, secretly broadcast
for a bizarre nationwide audience
of interested voyeurs and kindly
psychopaths, *but you couldn't've*
told me then, I wouldn't've known
that then, I pushed the weakest boy
in fifth grade, the so-skinny-he-looks-
sickly kid, John Muhovich, oldest
of a giant clan of poor kids, *yes*
that's his real name, I always use
real names in my poems, and in this way,
noticeably anxiety-ridden and singling out
the weak for especially attentive
oppression, I remind myself of most
of our politicians, *the whole damn*
caviar-choking chamber of Senators
enriching themselves, decrying
the work ethic of the poor when an extra
$300 in unemployment is enough to keep
sensible citizens home in this everlasting
decade of trauma and futility *and*
humankind-as-train-wreck-in-slow-motion

for years and years after that
schoolyear I only heard the name
John Muhovich once, on regional
network television news, a stepfather,
his ex's new man, had beaten John's child
so severely the child died, and I wanted
to call him right then and there and
apologize, not for his ever-resting child,
that wasn't my fault, but for being cruel
and stupid and for treating him
like he would never belong,
which every one of us were eager to do,
in that Catholic school they taught us
Blessed Are the Poor but close up
they tended to smell bad, one year

25

on the last day of school *I think*
it was the year the Martinez boy kicked
the over-friendly fat kid in the head
my so-called best friend who was more
of a personal bully, a bully providing
concierge-level service, sat outside
on a plastic schoolchair because we were
tasked with washing the furniture, *any*
damn thing to keep us busy
when the worksheets have run out,
and John Muhovich snuck up behind
the boy and yanked the chair out from under
him so he fell on his ass, *like a magician*
yanking a tablecloth out from under
a table setting except my bully boy went
down boom on his ass but the reason
he sat there not contributing to the labor
force was because he'd jumped off the swings
at the apex of his flight during recess
a couple hours earlier and landed directly on an arm,
which was probably broken, and he cried out
when John pulled the chair and cackled
with that weird bizarre laugh that we also
assumed must have something to do
with him being poor, and one of the
sister mary holy water holy rosary incantators,
one of the good girls, I mean, went "John!"
and we publicly abhorred him, collectively
and personally, tut-tutting and how-could-you-ing
and generally preening and showing off the most
moral of our peacock spread of feathers
because John wasn't being meek, *and we*
weren't about to let him get away with
inheriting the Earth.

Wondering

For the first time
in over 5 years   I wonder
how it might've been   if
it had worked out   She didn't kill herself
two weeks after we agreed
I'll take the kids all week
and she, the weekends   what if
she might've flourished   painting
making more and more paintings
and Dave, who was selling her paintings
for a cut of the money   was successful
in selling her paintings   and she lived
and painted   and took the kids   on the weekends

What if it didn't take her death to make me
more than a part time dad   what if I was not forced
by circumstance   to accept my responsibilities
but rather   came to them willingly   without drowning
in alcohol first   without my life requiring of me
something I'd given up on   having taken the mantle
not only out of necessity   but also out of   volition?

The thing is   I wished she would've stayed   and painted
I wish she could be there   in June   when Zaya graduates
I wish I would've done something   to keep her here
for the kids   without punishing her   for our failures
without condemning her   for the divorce
which was just   as much mine   as hers

Dad

I was not the boy
you'd've liked for me to be.

That would be junior,
the point guard.

I recollect feeling singular
and valued on a day you took me
to the field adjacent to Sacred
Heart to catch a football.

I never did ask to join
a football team. Once,
watching my younger brother play
and watching me watch him,
you turned to me and said,
"you know, it's not too late."

You would have to have
inhabited your body or mine
in that moment, knowing
what you saw in my face
and what you meant for me
to understand, as I do now,
that it was a gesture
of unfathomably gentle tenderness.

Uncle Buzz

I was adopted
by a family that tried
to raise me
in its image. Briefly,
they wanted me
to be one of them.

A patriarch, Uncle
Buzz, tried to show me
how to shoot an Uzi
but I had it on my
hip bone rather than against
soft flesh, and cried out,
then wept, when it kicked.

Buzz had an arsenal
locked up in the basement.
He showed us Ham
radio, said he never
lets them know quite
where he's at.

When he tried to show
us boys how to do a kip
and I placed my party-
favor whoopee-cushion
under him, he landed
on it. It burst.

I didn't want to
shoot a fucking gun
in the first place.

Old Buddy & Q

When we first knocked down
the kitchen wall and put the bar
and stools out, my bestie
would come over and we'd sit
and stare at sports on tv
just like we would at the bar.
I got sober and my buddy didn't.
The last time he came over
he told me that his QAnon
pals were trying to make things
right. Said he saw a drone
flying back and forth right above
his house, thought he had some idea
what that was all about. I tell myself
it's time to start praying for him.
The problem is you can't tell him
anything. He knows. He already knows.

Going On

Today I finished
In Evil Hour
by G.G. Marquez
hoping it would teach
me something about
fighting fascism
at the local level.

In Tennessee
they're burning books.

The ridiculous Purple
for Parents slander
social emotional learning
& anything else they
dislike as "Marxist."

A professional teacher
& writer in Indianapolis
suggests our state's public
education system is on
the verge of collapse.

I reviewed one good
book of poems yesterday,
like trying to catch
a flame in this windstorm
at the end of the world.

Dependability

If there's one motherfucking thing
I can rely on it's that the dogs
will bark at anything that moves
past the front window. Joggers,
kids on bikes, cats, the wavering
of tree branches, a bird
attacking a different bird,
squirrels, chipmunks, possums,
bumblebees, wasps, energy
stains of restless ghosts,
the kids' grandmothers,
one of those trucks driving around
with a Trump flag tossing in the wind
out the tail end lighting black cats
and chucking them out the passenger
side window on the 4th of *Joo-lai*,
runners in one of those walks
for charity or 5K's for charity
they route down the greenway
and up through the neighborhood
from time to time — that's a condensed list —
and I hate, hate hate hate,
hate how I have to yell at them
to quit barking as if the only
show of force their maniacal
impromptu neighborhood watch
respects is a louder more histrionic
and even more out of control bark back.

Evolution Christ

Evolution Christ explains
the multitudes of creatures;
in the modern translation
instructs us not to
eat them. His toes: webbed
in solidarity w/ ducks.
He spins silk straight
out the abdomen.
Evolution Christ is a hybrid
of mammal + super
power — he can kick
a Thundercat's ass.
He struts Darwin Way
singing, "Baby, don'chu
do it." Evolution Christ
is always cadging cigs
then putting a finger to
his lips like *Shhhhh,*
don't tell. He hasn't eaten
a hamburger in years.
When he makes love
the good earth erupts.

Meditation

… I tried to listen to the hum
of the refrigerator to stop
the river of words, eyes closed

meditating and listening
to the dog exhale as she slept
on the couch, a fat lump
of aerating mammal and

I described it in my head in
a river of words — I breathed
in and out making the Yah-
weh sound which is the name
of God — air in, air out and

I tried to connect with God
in this manner, felt it
in my skin in a contortion
of emotions, I tried

to calm my nips and chip
my dips and slip psychological
tricks into serene self-hypnosis,

stupid waking daydreams
crowding in, about making
sandwich jokes with an
old-timer recovery friend…

I Met This Anachronistic Hair Rock Guy Who Called Himself Frog in 1995 and Referred to This Problem as "Skin-Starved" as if That was the General Term for it in the Hair Rock World

"Get a massage" I'm often told
when the lack of touch in my life
seems more than I am able
to bear. But they don't
understand: nothing could make me hate
myself more than paying a stranger
for a backrub. Might as well
frequent the strip club at that point
which I also would not be able to
not feel ashamed of. Today,
I prayed. I ate an avocado
with chips. I ate a banana.
I had a Coke on the way
to pick up Zaya. I got
a new coffeemaker at Zaya's request.
I put Luke's PE clothes in the wash
even though I didn't feel like
getting my ass out of my chair
and going to the basement. I took
my anti-psychotic. I took two Ibuprofen.
None of it helped me feel
any better. I'm defective. There's a flaw
in my design. I feel too human or not
human enough. Not sure which.
All I know is, no one's laid hands
on me for months. Not lover.
Neither masseuse nor Priest.
No mother, no pastor, no therapist.
And I have this craving. It's awkward.
And I don't want to be ashamed of it.

Theology

Some people have poetry,
Some people have pickleball,
But both golf and Pokémon Go
Can be the ruination of a good
Walk. Considering how many
Folks fail to find meaning in church
Services, I'm inclined to question
The rate of return on a tithe.
Ten percent, that's all it takes
For some people to be sure
Of their place in the Whole
Wide Universe.

The Certified Land-Loving Poet of Reverence Speaks

Having gone this far into a minor
if mildly inspired avocation
as an unknown poet without
mentioning the landscape of this
my northern Indiana homeland
as it were, probably because —
heresy of poetic heresies:
I haven't really seen it.

My predictable proletarian excuse is
I'm not rich. We didn't live
on one of the lakes. I neither
fished nor swam. Nor are we
on one of the jankier lo-budget lakes
occupying our own in a cute
little cluster of trailers. Rather,
I'm in an older neighborhood not far
from the cemetery.

There are trees, I am aware of that,
deciduous and evergreen.
Our very own maple shoots
helicopters across the driveway
in spring and one of those awful

Callery Pears whose blooms smell
like semen, or toilet, spreads
its carnage on the lawn, committing
unnatural atrocities underground
with root-fingers creeping into the buried
poop-chute like *It* collecting children
in the sewer. All of this is real —

you and I know it, because
we live here, we've detected it.
I've gotten out my binoculars, I'm
on the case, *Encyclopedia Brown!*

I know what the sky looks like.
You can't argue with that
as long as we don't argue
about it. Sometimes I sit
in the backyard by the fire box
and sneeze. Most nights — more
often than not, anyway —
I notice the moon.

Calculations

My clan consists of accountants.
Living in the abstract.
Living in a world of Math.
I hate to travel

very far down the line
of thinking where everything
ends up made of Math.

It's like admitting
there's not much more to
the best poems you've ever read
than ink marks on paper.

a ma   f equati
   ze o   o
              n
            s under
     l
    y   ike
   ing it all l   we're
playing some sort of comp-
licated multi-dimensional Tetris.

How to differentiate between
what seems in the world and
what I know in my head.

This labor a kind of Calculus,
which I failed as a youth,
but the poor and kindly teacher
gave me a C.

They told me
God prefers checkers
to chess. Some days
I'm like, okay, sure.
Others, I think: not likely.

Okay

I'm learning to be okay.
It's a quiet marvel.
Sit and breathe. Eat some
almonds. Read a book.

I don't mind as much
when the world moves
slowly. I sit with stillness.

I despair like anyone.
Mostly due to loneliness. I love

poets and writers but a person
in a book is not a person
you can talk to. I am learning
to pray, which is also not

a person, quite, not one
directly talking to you.
But One you can talk to.
Then wait. Listen.

Dear God, I say,
like I'm writing a letter.
How are You? Bless
everyone. Please help
me. Us. Help us too.

III. The Most Sincere

Inspirational Speaker

I thought I'd let some cool air in
to the classroom so I opened the door
but the kids in the hall are noisy
and we're all gonna die.

We're reading Scott Russell Sanders
about his alcoholic father and
going where the pain is and
we're all gonna die.

We got banana splits for Teacher
Appreciation Week today.
We're all gonna die.

The kids share journals about
their tight meaningful relationships
with teachers in other departments
I can't say it makes me jealous but *anyway*
we're all gonna die.

The clock is ticking to the end
of the schoolyear, the beginning of summer, refreshing,
like a breath mint, we're all gonna die.

I've got no reason not to live
just like I've got no reason
to be depressed I've got an oriole
in my chest   the dull knife
of my heart   saws at my insides
it will portion me   into bite-sized pieces
from within   without.

Taking the Kids to See their Mother's Paintings

I was the one insisting
decisions ought to be made
about which pieces would be
kept, which sold — and — as
Dave at the gallery reminded me —
at what cost? So we got into
the minivan, the oldest next to me,
the two middle children in the middle
and our youngest boy in back, and
rode silently through the Winona stoplight,
down Pierceton Road to the Blue Pearl
and stood around in the first room
of the shop while Dave told our kids
all the things he'd already told me
about the situation of their mother's
paintings — I noticed the one
I had stared and stared at when I
came out earlier had disappeared —
after that first visit, I pulled away alone
in the Sienna and cried all the way
back home, but this time there were
no tears, not from the kids nor me,
though Dave choked up once talking
about how she'd almost turned the
corner into making a living with
her art alone, it shames me,
how close she came without my help,
not even really taking after it seriously
until we split, which also suggests
I was a problem, and I remember
in those last weeks we'd talked about
how with me taking the kids all weekdays
now, she'd have lots of time to paint,
to make it, to be okay, and she sort of
circled her head around instead of nodding,
said, ". . . yeah, really," as if she wasn't
quite sure, as if perhaps she had
something else planned.

Naner Poem

I like a young banana.
This is not a sexual euphemism.
A too-ripe banana ain't worth
chompin. Banana bread Schmanana
bread. I do like it though.
If somebody else makes it.

a Confession (35 years too late)

I talk about my gradeschool
bully-best-frenemy person
as if I never did a thing
wrong, but that's not true, listen:

once we went to a bookstore
to get candy and baseball cards
and we stole a lot — a *lot* —
of packs of basketball and football cards

from under the clerk's smellblind
nose, literally, right below her
as she schlumped behind the register,
and so his mother, the one who left us

at the bookstore in the first place
because errands are insufferable
and there's nothing in the minivan to steal,
called my mother once it was discovered

and said *the boys stole all these trading*
cards from ReadMore Books it must be
Mark's fault, it must be my boy's fault,
but I tell you what: Mark didn't

carry it off without an accomplice,
a willing one, yours truly, even if
by the time we got into the minivan
most of the packs of cards would remain

in his possession — you see when my mother
questioned me about it I was supposed to admit
my fault, accept my punishment and regret the error
of my ways but for some reason I can't fathom

to this day my mother reiterated his mother's
gracious and untrue claim of my innocence,
and I thought yeah, it must be all his fault,
he corrupted me, the Devil made me do it.

All the day long and the next and the next
no consequences were meted for my role
in the matter and I did not readily confess
leaving him to bear the brunt from his own

mother and perhaps that was when my friend
began to understand I wasn't much of a friend
in one way or more, just like he wasn't
much of a friend in other ways, for me.

Apocalypse 99

My apocalypse will always be the spring
and summer of 1999. Even my ex-wife's death
by suicide doesn't trump it. If you want proof
I can point to how I followed it with 17 solid years
of increasingly self-destructive alcoholism.
It's still not easy to think about. Still unresolved.
Because in some ways I'll always be scarred
and wearied from the memories of that year.
Of my suicide attempt. Of my half-assed
recovery. And in other ways I can't even be
counted among the ones who genuinely paid the price.

Self-Hypnosis

What's the point in figuring myself out
while the world burns?
Seems kind of precious. If only I knew
how much of it was really my fault.
I don't mean to suggest I am
a Very Important Man. I do wish
to have taken a vow of silence around
age 6, in 1982, or -3, & to have stead-
fastly stuck to it. Back then my parents
held a birthday party because it scared them
how I wasn't making any friends at school.
A kid in the kitchen poking at my floating
goldfish. They replaced it before the end
of the day, and, like I would so often
in the future, I pretended
a miracle occurred. I'm suspicious
even when it isn't called for, can you blame
me? What in the ever-lovin-fuck happened
to baby-me, anyway? Dropped on my head.
Switched at birth. Case of mistaken identity.
They tried to abandon me one time
in a Fort Lauderdale motel, but I screamed
until they decided I would never take a nap
now, magic fingers or no. I might've been four years old
when that happened. I bet you don't believe me.

Autobiography of My Body

I have a crunchy right ankle,
Broke it coming down from a dunk
On an 8-foot rim
Been crunchy ever since.
Heroically returned to travel soccer
Six weeks after breaking it
Scored a good goal at the White River State Games
Took a knee in the gut at full speed
And briefly couldn't breathe.
They call that "getting the wind
Knocked out of you." My body's felt
A lot worse. I don't know how much
Of it I'm going to tell you here.
Some of it's kinda personal.
I was an athlete through age 18,
19, then I was a depressed stoner,
Then I hit the road. I once left
Friends in a cold rainforest in Alaska
While I went looking for pot. I found it
And when I got back, no one wanted
To smoke it with me. My body can be
A selfish prick. It never learned to eat
Right. It still survives on a dull
Persistent sugar craving sated every few hours.
It's been addicted to alcohol.
It took Rohypnol on purpose 3 or 4 times.
That's because of its aloneness,
Not because I wanted to assault myself.
They used to call masturbation "self-
Abuse" and if that's what it is my body
Abused itself daily all through middle school,
Sometimes two, sometimes three times.
My body was sad and anxious and I know
Now, just by picking it up online,
Because I don't talk to my therapist
About my 8th grade masturbation habits,
That it was a manner of self-soothing.
My body seems like it's always been
Never not lonely. My mind

Insists I'd go ahead and be me again
If I had a do-over but my body
Sometimes hates itself. My body learned
So late in life that sex can't solve anything.
I want to say my body forgave me
For not knowing but the truth is
My body remembers everything.
My body, by virtue of including me
From the neck up, carries these old
Experiences day after day and can't let go
Of them and doesn't know how to let go.
If I told you, once, in captivity,
My body had the swollen abdomen
Of the starving Ethiopians of my
National Geographic childhood
Would you believe me? You probably
Wouldn't believe me, but my body knows.
You can't fool it. It wasn't supposed
To last past 1999, actually wasn't supposed
To live this long, and who knows how long it has.
I'm plump with visceral fat and
A fatty liver — I could go anytime.
Even though I've long since quit drinking.
I would like to say thank you to my body
For enduring all my stupidity,
My bad choices, all the harm
I put it through. But my body would probably
Be like, Ha. Yeah, right. Anytime, fucko.
What else can I do ya fer?

Slurry Cleanse

So I start running into this guy
at the bar I go to on non-kid days after work,
old buddy of my older brother, nice guy, still lives here
in the town where we grew up, like me.
We talk about food, his work, my work, his family,
my family, pop culture, politics, religion, whatever
          —   it's cool. I dig. I like the guy alright.
But the last time he popped up on the stool beside mine
at the Downtown, he busts out with, or rather he mutters
fast, as the fast mutter appears to be his preferred method
of utterance — "I'mgonnadoa slurrycleanse,
yousitinthisslurry, this allnaturalmixture,
takesallthe toxinsoutofyourbody, it even takes care
of your colon, Iknow, you'relaughing, it'sweird, Igetit,
but they gave me half off. I'm gonna try it, it
takes3hours, theytellmeafterwardsI'llfeelgreat."
And I do laugh, I can't help laughing,
trying to imagine what kind of hippy mumbo-jumbo
goes into whatever vat of all-natural ingredients he plans
to immerse himself in — nothing against hippies, I like hippies,
at least the one's with jobs, like Ben and Jerry, but it kinda makes
    me wonder,
if they have jobs, are they still hippies? BUT ANYWHO
I imagine this sludge of blueberry skins, flaxseed oil,
banana peels, shredded Tarot cards, oil of bergamot, eye
of newt, stuff like that — one can only imagine
the healing powers of beeswax, sea salt, locust husks, dead dictator
mustache hairs ... the conversation moved on, but later, after
I'd come home to let the dog out and turn up records loud enough
to make the house feel less empty, which is a volume that can't
    really be reached,
I have this flashback-epiphany. Wait. Hold on. "It even takes care
    of your colon?"
My man is gonna sit in a tub of vegetable juices Wiccan sweat and
    fossilized
Mastodon DNA for three hours and it will EVEN EVACUATE HIS
    COLON
and this is supposed to be a pleasant sensation, stewing in his own
    solids
among the various liquids, letting that septic cocktail mix and
    fume by the hour,

in this pig schwill mudbath of his own excrement and certifiably
   organic non-GMO
watermelon seeds? He'll come out smelling like he just met up
   with Pepe LePew
at a big city bathhouse. I might try it too, though. I mean, hell, for
   half off.

Trump Hands

I don't like my thumbs. They are small,
and weird. They are Donald Trump thumbs.
I have Donald Trump hands. Someone
surgically attached President Trump's hands
to my wrists. I'll never tip generously
again. These hands. So tiny. I disturb myself.
I can't even be stupidly arrogant about my height
(6'1") with these goddamned piddling things.
Yes, I know what they say about guys
with small hands which is a hilarious thing
to direct at President Trump but I need you
to know that's not helping me right now.
Are finger-lengtheners a thing?
Could I modify a penis enlargement device?
Would that be the end of me, or at least minimally
the beginning of a gruesome horrible mistake?
I don't even work with these hands. It's true.
I'm just like President Trump. I scribble
unintelligibly and I tweet out what I think
are Very Important Things to Say
with these goofy li'l' fingies. Oh Lord Great Pumpkin
Please Don't Turn Me Into Donald Trump!
Please, narrative arc of my life,
do not inform the audience that I was bit on
the shoulder by a radioactive Donald Trump
on a tour of anywhere but a library and I am now
doomed to develop the superpowers of bloviation,
bankruptcy, and infidelity. I feel like
the 2nd-safest man way down near the bottom
of Vlad Putin's hit list. Too useful to throw
out a window or spike my hospital applesauce
with an isotope. Please, if I start calling everything
beautiful, bragging about how I am the superior
practitioner of every last fucking activity
in the Universe, you should probably think hard
about putting me out of my misery.

New Underwear

I got new underwear
it was way overdue
like a library book

brand is And One
kind of a sheeny fabric
too sleek, considering
I never undress
for anyone

if my foot catches
in a leghole
after a shower
the things will stretch
all the way up
to my waist

The problem is
when I wear
these sheeny sumbitches
with khakis at
my place of employment

which is a school
sometimes one side
will get caught up
in the folds
of my upper thigh

& just under my ballsaq
riding into the general area
of my gluteus split

I can't mess with my pants
right there in the classroom
without looking like a lunatic
so I wait til a passing period
or lunch if I don't have time

to shimmy them sumbitches
down around mid thigh
where honest Christians
position them

sitting behind my desk
wondering if I'll ever get
this damn fabric
out of my asscrack
it's disconcerting,
to say the least

When it happens
it consumes me
there is nothing else
I can think of
til I set it right

Letter to my Eldest Children

for the older two, especially

It is a little after 10 a.m.,
Labor Day, and I'm thinking
of both of you. Remember
those parties your mom and I
used to throw on this holiday?
Hours of drinking, friends,
burgers, potatoes and bell peppers
in foil on the grill, and
the blustery, loud way
the men would talk
the longer we drank.

You must not've known
in the younger years, not all
dads got drunk, not all dads
shouted at each other with
sauced political passion on
white plastic patio furniture
in the back yard. For a long
time, it never occurred to me
I ought to live differently.
By the time I came to,
The eldest was halfway out the door,
on to art school, your mother
ashes in a box at your grandma's house,
a memory the younger of you
never mentioned, while, even
as I sobered up, I failed
egregiously at paying
sufficient attention.

I wish I knew the right words
to ask forgiveness for us,
your parents. I know you
handled more than children
should ever be expected to.

That tree we planted for
your mom with the teachers
and the kids from your
elementary school, in the back
yard, was struck by lightning
early spring this year.
It surprised us when
a couple clusters of leaves
sprouted further down on the
trunk, below the deadened
and nearly detached part.
It lived. It went on living.
No one expected it to.

Not every living thing
can persevere. It's no one's
fault, though if it is, it's mine,
not yours. I'm sorry for my part
in what you've both been through.
I'm sorry for the foolishness,
for the selfish things I've done.

Dissociation

Some things cannot be talked about.
The last time I saw my father
lying on the living room floor.
How I sat at my bedroom desk
unable to concentrate on Driver's Ed
homework repeating in my head
I didn't need to run through the woods
to the hospital on the other side
of the neighborhood. Mom said
this was nothing so it would be nothing.
Any moment now, back to our regularly
scheduled life. Any minute now, back
to our regularly scheduled program.
Some moments I live again.
So many moments when nothing happened.
Confined in Bloomington I was sure
I would be beaten. I waited for it. I didn't
do anything. It was like they expected me
to acquiesce. We want to punish you
and we want you to want your punishment.
Crave it. Lick it up like spilt whiskey
on the hardwood floor. Nothing happened.
Nothing ever happens again and again.
When he died it was nothing. And she,
she was nothing. Another trick, another actor
playing a role to provoke a response.
Another cipher in this matrix of sorcery,
this joke of a life the gods gave me.
But I do love the children she gave me.
Spare them. Spare them, oh God,
If it is true that You are Good, because
I want to believe it, to believe
in You. Spare my children. I do love them so.

Acknowledgements

On A Day I'm Wondering, Any American High School .... *Trailer Park Quarterly*

Latte Interlude, Awareness Level: Eleven, Okay, Inspirational Speaker . . . . *Panoply Michiana*

Adult Basic Education . . . . *Up North*

Wondering, Theology, The Certified Land Loving Poet of Reverence Speaks . . . . *Indianapolis Review*

Dad . . . . *Anti-Heroin Chic*

Old Buddy & Q . . . . *New York Quarterly*

Going On . . . . *Genuine Gold*

Dependability . . . . *Harpur Palate*

Evolution Christ . . . *Into the Void*

Calculations . . . . *Quibble*

Taking the Kids to See . . . . . *Hole in the Head Review*

Naner Poem . . . . . *Brave Voices*

Slurry Cleanse . . . . *Rattle*

Fort Wayne Sport Club Travel Soccer... *The Under Review*

a Funeral, Raised on Grease and Child Abuse, Uncle Buzz . . . *Misfit*

High School English Teacher . . . *Porcupine Literary*

Hail Mary, Bob-O-Matic and Jack's Gettin Up There appeared in the chapbook *American Male* (Main Street Rag 2022)

Dissociation appeared in the chapbook *Guilty Prayer* (Main Street Rag 2021)

Biography

Steve Henn is in his 22nd year teaching high school English in northern Indiana. His other recent collection, *Deep Cuts*, will be published soon by Wolfson Press. Additional books can be found at Wolfson, Main Street Rag, and NYQ Books. Check out therealstevehenn.com for reading news, links to books and poems, etc. May God have mercy on Steve & us all.

www.ingramcontent.com/pod-product-compliance
Lightning Source LLC
Chambersburg PA
CBHW071357090426
42738CB00012B/3148